**TEACHER'S PET PUBLICATIONS**

LITPLAN TEACHER PACK
for
A Doll's House
based on the play by
Henrik Ibsen

Written by
Mary B. Collins

© 1994 Teacher's Pet Publications
All Rights Reserved

This **LitPlan** for Henrik Ibsen's
A Doll's House
has been brought to you by Teacher's Pet Publications, Inc.

Copyright Teacher's Pet Publications 1994

Only the student materials in this unit plan
such as worksheets, study questions, assignment sheets, and tests
may be reproduced multiple times for use in the purchaser's classroom.

For any additional copyright questions,
contact Teacher's Pet Publications.

www.tpet.com

TABLE OF CONTENTS - *A Doll's House*

Introduction	5
Unit Objectives	7
Reading Assignment Sheet	8
Unit Outline	9
Study Questions (Short Answer)	13
Quiz/Study Questions (Multiple Choice)	17
Pre-reading Vocabulary Worksheets	25
Lesson One (Introductory Lesson)	35
Nonfiction Assignment Sheet	51
Oral Reading Evaluation Form	40
Writing Assignment 1	37
Writing Assignment 2	50
Writing Assignment 3	53
Writing Evaluation Form	54
Vocabulary Review Activities	47
Extra Writing Assignments/Discussion ?s	44
Unit Review Activities	55
Unit Tests	59
Unit Resource Materials	87
Vocabulary Resource Materials	101

A FEW NOTES ABOUT THE AUTHOR
Henrik Ibsen

IBSEN, Henrik (1828-1906). The first great modern playwright was Henrik Ibsen, a Norwegian. His plays show a wide variety of styles, ranging from the realism of 'Hedda Gabler' to the fantasy of 'Peer Gynt'. He is admired for his technical mastery, symbolism, and deep psychological insight.

Ibsen, born on March 20, 1828, in the small port town of Skien, Norway, was one of six children. When the boy was eight, his father went bankrupt. For the next eight years the family lived on a small farm near Skien. At 15 Ibsen was apprenticed to a druggist in the town of Grimstadt. It was a lonely life, and the boy soon turned to writing, especially poetry.

In 1849 Ibsen entered the university at Christiania (now Oslo), but he soon dropped out for lack of money. His life was hard for many years. He did routine writing for newspapers and managed a small theater. He traveled in Germany and Denmark to study scene design. He also wrote poetry and unsuccessful plays.

Finally in 1864, aided by a small government grant and the help of friends, Ibsen left Norway to live in Rome, Italy. His first successful play, 'Brand', was originally written in 1865 as a narrative poem. Recast as a drama, it was first performed in 1885. It tells the grim story of a minister who renounces the compromises of his time in favor of a "true-to-oneself" life. His next play was 'Peer Gynt' (1867), the tale of a world traveler involved in a variety of remarkable adventures. Wild as the story is, its point is clear-that a second-rate life has little meaning and purpose.

Then followed 'The League of Youth' (1868), about political corruption, and 'Emperor and Galilean' (1873), a plea for a new kind of Christianity. 'The Pillars of Society' (1877) and 'A Doll's House' (1879) deal with social reforms based on the principles of honesty and freedom. 'Ghosts' (1881), about the tragedy of disease that affects the mind, is perhaps Ibsen's greatest play.

Among his later plays are 'An Enemy of the People' (1882), a comedy with serious undertones; 'The Wild Duck' (1884), combining reality and poetry; and 'Rosmersholm' (1886), dealing with the conflict between conscience and desire for freedom. 'Hedda Gabler' (1890) is a powerful domestic tragedy ending in suicide. Among his last plays are 'The Master Builder' (1892) and 'When We Dead Awaken' (1899).

After years of living alternately in Rome and Dresden and Munich, Germany, Ibsen returned to Norway in 1892. He was rich, honored by the world, and loved by his own people. His plays were translated into many languages and staged in countries all over the world. He died in Christiania on May 23, 1906.

--- Courtesy of Compton's Learning Company

INTRODUCTION

This unit has been designed to develop students' reading, writing, thinking, and language skills through exercises and activities related to *A Doll's House* by Henrik Ibsen. It includes seventeen lessons, supported by extra resource materials.

The **introductory lesson** introduces students to the play through a writing activity. Following the introductory activity, students are given a transition to explain how the activity relates to the play they are about to read. Following the transition, students are given the materials they will be using during the unit. .

The **reading assignments** are approximately thirty pages each; some are a little shorter while others are a little longer. Students have approximately 15 minutes of pre-reading work to do prior to each reading assignment. This pre-reading work involves reviewing the study questions for the assignment and doing some vocabulary work for 8 to 10 vocabulary words they will encounter in their reading.

The **study guide questions** are fact-based questions; students can find the answers to these questions right in the text. These questions come in two formats: short answer or multiple choice. The best use of these materials is probably to use the short answer version of the questions as study guides for students (since answers will be more complete), and to use the multiple choice version for occasional quizzes. If your school has the appropriate equipment, it might be a good idea to make transparencies of your answer keys for the overhead projector.

The **vocabulary work** is intended to enrich students' vocabularies as well as to aid in the students' understanding of the play. Prior to each reading assignment, students will complete a two-part worksheet for approximately 8 to 10 vocabulary words in the upcoming reading assignment. Part I focuses on students' use of general knowledge and contextual clues by giving the sentence in which the word appears in the text. Students are then to write down what they think the words mean based on the words' usage. Part II nails down the definitions of the words by giving students dictionary definitions of the words and having students match the words to the correct definitions based on the words' contextual usage. Students should then have an understanding of the words when they meet them in the text.

After each reading assignment, students will go back and formulate answers for the study guide questions. Discussion of these questions serves as a **review** of the most important events and ideas presented in the reading assignments.

In this unit the play is read orally with different students taking the parts of the characters. There is a **Speaking Part Assignment Sheet** which lists the parts and leaves a place for you to fill in students' names.

After students complete reading the work, there is a **vocabulary review** lesson which pulls together all of the fragmented vocabulary lists for the reading assignments and gives students a review of all of the words they have studied.

A lesson is devoted to the **extra discussion questions/writing assignments**. These questions focus on interpretation, critical analysis and personal response, employing a variety of thinking skills and adding to the students' understanding of the play.

There are three **writing assignments** in this unit, each with the purpose of informing, persuading, or having students express personal opinions. The first assignment is to express personal opinions: students tell what they think a woman's role should be in our society. The second assignment is to persuade: students create two advertisements they believe they would find in a playbill. The third assignment is to inform: students create a playbill for *A Doll's House*.

In addition, there is a **nonfiction reading assignment**. Students are required to read a piece of nonfiction related in some way to *A Doll's House*. After reading their nonfiction pieces, students will fill out a worksheet on which they answer questions regarding facts, interpretation, criticism, and personal opinions. During one class period, students make **oral presentations** about the nonfiction pieces they have read. This not only exposes all students to a wealth of information, but it also gives students the opportunity to practice **public speaking**.

The **review lesson** pulls together all of the aspects of the unit. The teacher is given four or five choices of activities or games to use which all serve the same basic function of reviewing all of the information presented in the unit.

The **unit test** comes in two formats: multiple choice or short answer. As a convenience, two different tests for each format have been included. There is also an advanced short answer test for students who need more challenge.

There are additional **support materials** included with this unit. The **extra activities section** includes suggestions for an in-class library, crossword and word search puzzles related to the play, and extra vocabulary worksheets. There is a list of **bulletin board ideas** which gives the teacher suggestions for bulletin boards to go along with this unit. In addition, there is a list of **extra class activities** the teacher could choose from to enhance the unit or as a substitution for an exercise the teacher might feel is inappropriate for his/her class. **Answer keys** are located directly after the **reproducible student materials** throughout the unit. The student materials may be reproduced for use in the teacher's classroom without infringement of copyrights. No other portion of this unit may be reproduced without the written consent of Teacher's Pet Publications, Inc.

UNIT OBJECTIVES - *A Doll's House*

1. Through reading Ibsen's *A Doll's House*, students will consider the role of women in society.

2. Students will demonstrate their understanding of the text on four levels: factual, interpretive, critical, and personal.

3. Students will determine and discuss the relationships among the characters.

4. Students will consider "law" versus "justice" and "legality" versus "morality."

5. Students will be given the opportunity to practice reading aloud and silently to improve their skills in each area.

6. Students will answer questions to demonstrate their knowledge and understanding of the main events and characters in *A Doll's House* as they relate to the author's theme development.

7. Students will enrich their vocabularies and improve their understanding of the play through the vocabulary lessons prepared for use in conjunction with the play.

8. The writing assignments in this unit are geared to several purposes:
    a. To have students demonstrate their abilities to inform, to persuade, or to express their own personal ideas

    > Note: Students will demonstrate ability to write effectively to <u>inform</u> by developing and organizing facts to convey information. Students will demonstrate the ability to write effectively to <u>persuade</u> by selecting and organizing relevant information, establishing an argumentative purpose, and by designing an appropriate strategy for an identified audience. Students will demonstrate the ability to write effectively to <u>express personal ideas</u> by selecting a form and its appropriate elements.

    b. To check the students' reading comprehension
    c. To make students think about the ideas presented by the play
    d. To encourage logical thinking
    e. To provide an opportunity to practice good grammar and improve students' use of the English language.

9. Students will read aloud, report, and participate in large and small group discussions to improve their public speaking and personal interaction skills.

READING ASSIGNMENT SHEET - *A Doll's House*

Date Assigned	Act Assigned	Completion Date
	One	
	Two	
	Three	

UNIT OUTLINE - *A Doll's House*

1	2	3	4	5
Introduction Writing Assignment #1	Part Assignments PV Act 1	Read Act 1	Study ?s Act 1 PV Act 2	Read Act 2
6 Study ?s Act 2 PV Act 3	**7** Read Act 3	**8** Study ?s Act 3 Extra ?s	**9** Extra ?s Discussion	**10** Vocabulary
11 Writing Assignment #2	**12** Library	**13** Reports	**14** Speaker	**15** Writing Assignment #3
16 Review	**17** Test			

Key: P=Preview Study Questions V=Prereading Vocabulary Worksheet R=Read

STUDY GUIDE QUESTIONS

SHORT ANSWER STUDY GUIDE QUESTIONS - *A Doll's House*

Act One
1. Describe the relationship between Nora and Helmer.
2. What is supposed to happen for Helmer at the beginning of the new year, and what will it mean for him and his family?
3. Who is Mrs. Linde, and why has she come back?
4. What was Nora's secret?
5. Who is Krogstad?
6. Who is Dr. Rank, and what is his problem?
7. How did Krogstad persuade Nora to try to influence Helmer on his behalf?
8. What crime had Krogstad committed, and what was Helmer's reaction to it?
9. Why doesn't Nora want to see her children at the end of Act One?

Act Two
1. What final arguments does Helmer make to Nora as reasons for firing Krogstad?
2. Nora was going to ask a favor of Dr. Rank, but she changed her mind. What was the favor, and why did she change her mind?
3. What was in Krogstad's letter to Helmer?
4. How does Mrs. Linde plan to help Nora?
5. By the end of Act Two, Nora has come to a decision. What is it?

Act Three
1. Why did Krogstad send the document back to Nora?
2. Why did Mrs. Linde tell Krogstad not to go get the letter back?
3. What was Helmer's reaction to Krogstad's letter?
4. What did Helmer do when he opened the envelope containing the document from Krogstad?
5. Why did Nora leave Helmer?

ANSWER KEY: SHORT ANSWER STUDY GUIDE QUESTIONS - *A Doll's House*

Act One

1. Describe the relationship between Nora and Helmer.
    Helmer is the breadwinner, the head of the household who takes care of Nora, who appears to be his rather spoiled playmate.

2. What is supposed to happen for Helmer at the beginning of the new year, and what will it mean for him and his family?
    He is supposed to get a promotion to be manager of the bank. It will mean more money and fewer money worries (particularly for Nora).

3. Who is Mrs. Linde, and why has she come back?
    She is one of Nora's old friends. She came to Nora in hopes of getting a job at the bank.

4. What was Nora's secret?
    She borrowed money to finance a trip south to Italy to save Torvald's life, and she never told him that she borrowed it. She has been making payments by skimming from the household money and taking in copying work.

5. Who is Krogstad?
    Krogstad is a lawyer who has a "subordinate" position at the bank (which Helmer is about to terminate). He has a reputation for being a shady character. Nora borrowed the money for the trip south from him.

6. Who is Dr. Rank, and what is his problem?
    He is a friend to Helmer and Nora. He has an illness we later discover is terminal, tuberculosis of the spine.

7. How did Krogstad persuade Nora to try to influence Helmer on his behalf?
    He threatened to tell Helmer about her loan and to make public the fact that she forged her father's signature on the note.

8. What crime had Krogstad committed, and what was Helmer's reaction to it?
    He also had committed forgery. Helmer told Nora how horrible Krogstad was, especially for lying and deceiving his own family--poisoning his own home.

9. Why doesn't Nora want to see her children at the end of Act One?
    Helmer has just told her how horrible deceit is and how it poisons the home and the children. She really doesn't want to hurt anyone or be a bad influence, so she avoids the children while she begins to face her problem.

Act Two
1. What final arguments does Helmer make to Nora as reasons for firing Krogstad?
   Helmer tells Nora that Krogstad calls him on a first-name basis at the office, reminding everyone of their past friendship; that looks bad for Helmer because of Krogstad's resent shady reputation. Besides, he has told everyone at the bank that Krogstad will be released; he would look ridiculous if he would change his mind.

2. Nora was going to ask a favor of Dr. Rank, but she changed her mind. What was the favor, and why did she change her mind?
   She was going to ask him to lend her the money to pay off her loan. Rank declared his love for her, and asking for the money just was not appropriate. She just couldn't bring herself to do it.

3. What was in Krogstad's letter to Helmer?
   He wrote an explanation of Nora's loan and the forgery to blackmail Helmer into letting him keep his job (and perhaps better his position) at the bank.

4. How does Mrs. Linde plan to help Nora?
   She wants to speak to Krogstad on Nora's behalf since she and Krogstad were once close friends.

5. By the end of Act Two, Nora has come to a decision. What is it?
   She has decided to commit suicide.

Act Three
1. Why did Krogstad send the document back to Nora?
   Mrs. Linde renewed her friendship with him and gave him hope for the future. He wanted a good, new life with her. He hadn't really wanted to hurt Nora and Helmer; he just couldn't see any other way to continue without a job or hope.

2. Why did Mrs. Linde tell Krogstad not to go get the letter back?
   "Helmer's got to learn everything; this dreadful secret has to be aired; those two have to come to a full understanding; all these lies and evasions can't go on."

3. What was Helmer's reaction to Krogstad's letter?
   He flies into a rage and calls Nora a criminal, a liar, a hypocrite, and disgusting. He forbids her to raise the children and says their marriage will be one only of appearances.

4. What did Helmer do when he opened the envelope containing the document from Krogstad?
   He instantly forgave Nora and said that everything would be as it was (only better because they will be closer because of Nora's weaknesses).

5. Why does Nora leave Helmer?

    She realizes that he is more concerned for himself and appearances than for her. He is not the man she thought he was. She has discovered the real world and wants to be a part of it, to educate herself and be a responsible individual instead of someone else's "doll."

MULTIPLE CHOICE STUDY GUIDE/QUIZ QUESTIONS - *A Doll's House*

<u>Act One</u>

1. True or False: Helmer and Nora have an egalitarian relationship. They both take equal responsibility in earning money and running the household.
    a. True
    b. False

2. What is supposed to happen for Helmer at the beginning of the New Year?
    a. He will come into an inheritance from his father.
    b. He will become a full partner in a law firm.
    c. He will get a promotion to be manager of the bank.
    d. He will get a commission in the Royal Navy.

3. Who is Mrs. Linde, and why has she come back?
    a. She is one of Nora's old friends. She has come to Nora in hopes that Helmer can help her get a job.
    b. She is Nora's father's former housekeeper. She has come with some letters and memorabilia that Nora's father had given her before he died.
    c. She is an old flame of Helmer's. Nora has committed herself to being polite for Helmer's sake, even though she doesn't really want Mrs. Linde in her house.
    d. She is a former teacher of Nora's. She has returned to start a school and wants Nora to enroll her children and persuade her friends to do the same.

4. What was Nora's secret?
    a. She was starting her own business and was slowly becoming successful. She didn't want Helmer to know about it until she had some profit to show him.
    b. She was pregnant again. She was afraid to tell Helmer because he said he already had enough mouths to feed.
    c. She was secretly in love with another man. She vowed never to act on her feelings because she didn't want to disrupt her family.
    d. She had borrowed the money to finance the trip to Italy to save Helmer's life. She has been making payments by skimming from the household money and taking in copy work.

5. Which of the following statements does not describe Krogstad?
    a. He is a lawyer who has a subordinate position at the bank.
    b. He is a former suitor of Nora's who is still in love with her.
    c. He has a reputation for being a shady character.
    d. He has loaned Nora money in the past.

A Doll's House Multiple Choice Study Questions Page 2

6. What is Dr. Rank's problem?
    a. He has terminal tuberculosis of the spine.
    b. He is going blind.
    c. He is bankrupt and is embarrassed to tell anyone.
    d. He had been secretly in love with Mrs. Linde many years ago. Now that she is back in the picture, he doesn't know what to do about it.

7. How did Krogstad persuade Nora to try to influence Helmer on his behalf?
    a. He offered her money.
    b. He "sweet-talked" her with compliments about her beauty and her influence over her husband.
    c. He begged her, playing on her sympathy because he was a widower trying to raise his children.
    d. He blackmailed her with his knowledge of something she had done several years earlier.

8. True or False: Krogstad had committed forgery. Helmer told Nora how horrible Krogstad was, especially for lying and deceiving his own family.
    a. True
    b. False

9. True or False: Nora decides not to see her children because she wants to devote all of her time to being a perfect wife for Helmer.
    a. True
    b. False

A Doll's House Multiple Choice Study Questions Page 3

Act Two

10. Which of the following is not one of the arguments that Helmer makes to Nora as reasons for firing Krogstad?
    a. Krogstad calls Helmer by his first name at the office, thus reminding everyone of their past friendship.
    b. He has already told everyone that Krogstad will be released.
    c. Krogstad has already secured another position, and it would look very bad for Krogstad if he were to back out on that now.
    d. It would make him (Helmer) look bad to change his mind.

11. True or False: Nora was planning to ask Dr. Rank to lend her the money to pay off her loan.
    a. True
    b. False

12. True or False: When Dr. Rank declared his love for her, she went ahead with her plan. She was sure he couldn't refuse her request.
    a. True
    b. False

13. True or False: Krogstad wrote a letter to Helmer explaining the loan and forgery to blackmail Helmer into letting him keep his job at the bank.
    a. True
    b. False

14. How does Mrs. Linde plan to help Nora?
    a. She is going to take in handwork and give half of the profits to Nora to help her pay off the loan.
    b. She is going to lend Nora some of her own money and let Nora pay her back.
    c. She is going to speak to Krogstad on Nora's behalf since they were once close friends.
    d. She is going to help Nora get more copying work so she can earn more money and repay the loan more quickly.

15. By the end of Act Two, Nora has come to a decision. What is it?
    a. She has decided to commit suicide.
    b. She has decided to tell Helmer the whole story and take the consequences.
    c. She had decided to kill Krogstad.
    d. She has decided to run away from home and never return.

A Doll's House Multiple Choice Study Questions Page 4

Act Three

16. True or False: Krogstad returned the documents to Nora after Mrs. Linde renewed her friendship with him and gave him hope for the future.
    a. True
    b. False

17. Why did Mrs. Linde tell Krogstad not to get the letter back?
    a. She wanted to keep it as security. That way she could never be fired from the bank since she would have the letter to use as blackmail.
    b. It was too late at night and very cold and stormy. Now that they were together again, she didn't want to risk losing him by having him fall ill from exposure to the weather.
    c. She thought that Torvald should know the truth so that everything could be brought out into the open and the air could be cleared.
    d. She thought it was too late, that Nora had already picked the lock and taken the letter. Going over now to retrieve it would only make matters worse.

18. What was Helmer's reaction to the letter.
    a. He flew into a rage and called Nora a criminal, a hypocrite, and a liar. He said she was not fit to raise their children and that their marriage would be one only of appearances.
    b. He refused to believe that his "Songbird" would do any such thing. He vowed to get even with Krogstad and have him permanently disgraced so that he would have to move far away if he ever wanted to get work again.
    c. He said he would stand up for Nora no matter what and that he would always love her.
    d. He started crying and then had a stroke.

19. What did Helmer do when he opened the envelope containing the document from Krogstad?
    a. He said it didn't make any difference, that Nora was still wrong and he would not forgive her.
    b. He instantly forgave her and said that everything would be even better than before because of Nora's weaknesses.
    c. He ran from the room.
    d. He slapped Nora.

20. What did Nora do at the end of the play.
    a. She went to bed and slept happily next to her husband.
    b. She left Helmer to go out and be a part of the real world and become a responsible individual.
    c. She committed suicide.
    d. She begged Helmer to keep her and promised to become a better wife.

ANSWER KEY - MULTIPLE CHOICE STUDY/QUIZ QUESTIONS
A Doll's House

Act One	Act Two	Act Three
1. B	10. C	16. A
2. C	11. A	17. C
3. A	12. B	18. A
4. D	13. A	19. B
5. B	14. C	20. B
6. A	15. A	
7. D		
8. A		
9. B		

PREREADING VOCABULARY WORKSHEETS

VOCABULARY - *A Doll's House* Act One

Part I: Using Prior Knowledge and Contextual Clues

Below are the sentences in which the vocabulary words appear in the text. Read the sentence. Use any clues you can find in the sentence combined with your prior knowledge, and write what you think the underlined words mean in the space provided.

1. But you know we can't go squandering.

2. No, the easy chair there! I'll take the rocker here. (Seizing her hands)

3. Oh, Kristine, you must believe me; I often thought of writing you then, but I kept postponing it, and something always interfered.

4. (looking incredulously at her)

5. My mother was still alive, but bedridden and helpless--and I had my two younger brothers to look after.

6. I could have gotten it from some admirer or other. After all, a girl with my ravishing appeal....

7. Is it indiscreet to save your husband's life?

8. He said I was frivolous, and it was his duty as man of the house not to indulge me in whims and fancies....

9. In the business world there's what they call quarterly interest and what they call amortization, and these are always so terribly hard to manage.

10. See here, macaroons! I thought they were contraband here.

A Doll's House Vocabulary Act One Continued

11. NORA (vehemently). But go on and try. It'll turn out the worse for you, because then my husband will really see what a crook you are, and then you'll *never* be able to hold your job.

12. Every breath the children take is filled with the germs of something degenerate.

Part II: Determining the Meaning

    You have tried to figure out the meanings of the vocabulary words for Act One. Now match the vocabulary words to their dictionary definitions. If there are words for which you cannot figure out the definition by contextual clues and by process of elimination, look them up in a dictionary.

___ 1. squandering   A. confined to bed due to illness
___ 2. seizing   B. illegal goods
___ 3. interfered   C. forcefully; full of strong emotions
___ 4. incredulously   D. extremely attractive
___ 5. bedridden   E. wasting money on extravagant purchases
___ 6. ravishing   F. with disbelief
___ 7. indiscreet   G. something having declined from a former state
___ 8. frivolous   H. prorating or spreading the repayment of debt over a period of time
___ 9. amortization   I. trivial; silly; unimportant
___10. contraband   J. grabbing; taking and holding
___11. vehemently   K. lacking discretion; injudicious
___12. degenerate   L. got in the way; hindered

Vocabulary - *A Doll's House* Act Two

Part I: Using Prior Knowledge and Contextual Clues
    Below are the sentences in which the vocabulary words appear in the text. Read the sentence. Use any clues you can find in the sentence combined with your prior knowledge, and write what you think the underlined words mean in the space provided.

1. NORA (walking more jauntily). Hmp! When you've had three children, then you've had a few visits from--from women who know something of medicine, and they tell you this and that.

2. How can a man of such refinement be so grasping?

3. What an intolerable situation that would have been!

4. Your father's official career was hardly above reproach.

5. I tell you, it's been excruciating for me. He's out to make my place in the bank unbearable.

6. And in every single family, in some way or another, this inevitable retribution of nature goes on....

7. For a year and a half I've kept myself clean of anything disreputable--all that time struggling with the worst conditions; but I was satisfied, working my way up step by step.

8. Now, now, now--no hysterics. Be my own little lark again.

9. Twenty-four hours to the midnight after, and then the tarantella's done.

Doll's House Vocabulary Act Two Continued

Part II: Determining the Meaning

You have tried to figure out the meanings of the vocabulary words for Act Two. Now match the vocabulary words to their dictionary definitions. If there are words for which you cannot figure out the definition by contextual clues and by process of elimination, look them up in a dictionary.

___ 13. jauntily   A. lacking respectability; shady
___ 14. refinement   B. agonizing; painful
___ 15. intolerable   C. emotional outbursts
___ 16. reproach   D. briskly; full of self-confidence
___ 17. excruciating   E. having good manners and social graces
___ 18. retribution   F. lively Italian dance
___ 19. disreputable   G. criticism
___ 20. hysterics   H. unbearable
___ 21. tarantella   I. justly deserved; punishment

Vocabulary - *A Doll's House* Act Three

Part I: Using Prior Knowledge and Contextual Clues
    Below are the sentences in which the vocabulary words appear in the text. Read the sentence. Use any clues you can find in the sentence combined with your prior knowledge, and write what you think the underlined words mean in the space provided.

1. Helmer's got to learn everything; this dreadful secret has to be aired; those two have to come to a full understanding; all these lies and <u>evasions</u> can't go on.

2. She danced her tarantella and got a <u>tumultuous</u> hand--which was well earned . . . .

3. Oh, no; I took my lovely little Capri girl--my <u>capricious</u> little Capri girl, I should say--took her under my arm; one quick tour of the ballroom, a curtsy to every side, and then--as they say in plays--the beautiful vision disappeared.

4. HELMER (<u>suppressing</u> a smile). Ah, of course.

5. NORA (with bewildered glances, groping about, seizing Helmer's <u>domino</u>, throwing it around her, and speaking in short, hoarse, broken whispers).

6. What is this you've <u>blundered</u> into!

7. In all these eight years--she who was my pride and joy--a <u>hypocrite</u>, a liar--worse, worse--a criminal!

8. NORA (<u>unperturbed</u>). I mean, then I went from Papa's hands into yours. You arranged everything to your own taste, and so I got the same taste as you--or I pretended to; I can't remember.

9. Oh, you blind, <u>incompetent</u> child!

10. But what good would my protests be against you? That was the miracle I was waiting for, in terror and hope. And to <u>stave</u> that off, I would have taken my life.

A Doll's House Vocabulary Act Three Continued

Part II: Determining the Meaning

You have tried to figure out the meanings of the vocabulary words for Act Three. Now match the vocabulary words to their dictionary definitions. If there are words for which you cannot figure out the definition by contextual clues and by process of elimination, look them up in a dictionary.

___ 22. evasions	A. holding down or holding back
___ 23. tumultuous	B. unruffled; not bothered; calmly
___ 24. capricious	C. costume with a hooded robe
___ 25. suppressing	D. avoiding
___ 26. domino	E. moved clumsily or stupidly into
___ 27. blundered	F. impulsive; whimsical, unpredictable
___ 28. hypocrite	G. hold off; keep away
___ 29. unperturbed	H. extremely noisy and disorderly
___ 30. incompetent	I. lacking abilities
___ 31. stave	J. one who says he believes one way nut whose actions show he believes another

ANSWER KEY: VOCABULARY - *A Doll's House*

Act One		Act Two		Act Three	
1.	E	13.	D	22.	D
2.	J	14.	E	23.	H
3.	L	15.	H	24.	F
4.	F	16.	G	25.	A
5.	A	17.	B	26.	C
6.	D	18.	I	27.	E
7.	K	19.	A	28.	J
8.	I	20.	C	29.	B
9.	H	21.	F	30.	I
10.	B			31.	G
11.	C				
12.	G				

DAILY LESSONS

LESSON ONE

Objectives
    1. To introduce the *Doll's House* unit
    2. To distribute books and other materials students will use in the unit
    3. To give students the opportunity to express their own opinions
    4. To give the teacher the opportunity to evaluate students' writing skills

Activity #1
    Distribute Writing Assignment #1. Discuss the directions in detail and give students ample time to complete the assignment.

Activity #2
    Distribute the materials students will use in this unit. Explain in detail how students are to use these materials.

    Study Guides   Students should read the study guide questions for each reading assignment prior to beginning the reading assignment to get a feeling for what events and ideas are important in the section they are about to read. After reading the section, students will (as a class or individually) answer the questions to review the important events and ideas from that section of the play. Students should keep the study guides as study materials for the unit test.

    Vocabulary   Prior to reading a reading assignment, students will do vocabulary work related to the section of the play they are about to read. Following the completion of the reading of the play, there will be a vocabulary review of all the words used in the vocabulary assignments. Students should keep their vocabulary work as study materials for the unit test.

    Reading Assignment Sheet   You need to fill in the reading assignment sheet to let students know by when their reading has to be completed. You can either write the assignment sheet up on a side blackboard or bulletin board and leave it there for students to see each day or you can "ditto" copies for each student to have. In either case, you should advise students to become very familiar with the reading assignments so they know what is expected of them.

    Extra Activities Center   The Extra Activities page of this unit contains suggestions for an extra library of related plays and articles in your classroom as well as crossword and word search puzzles. Make an extra activities center in your room where you will keep these materials for students to use. (Bring the plays and articles in from the library and keep several copies of the puzzles on hand.) Explain to students that these materials are available for students to use when they finish reading assignments or other class work early.

<u>Nonfiction Assignment Sheet</u> Explain to students that they each are to read at least one non-fiction piece from the in-class library at some time during the unit. Students will fill out a nonfiction assignment sheet after completing the reading to help you evaluate their reading experiences and to help the students think about and evaluate their own reading experiences.

WRITING ASSIGNMENT #1 - *A Doll's House*

PROMPT

In Ibsen's play, *A Doll's House*, the main character, Nora, is forced to look at her life--her roles as a person, a mother, a wife, a worker. Even though the play was published in the late 1870s, the ideas Ibsen explores are still quite appropriate for people today.

Your assignment is to answer the question, "What is a woman's role in society?" In what area(s) do a woman's most important responsibilities lie? The topic is intentionally vague to give you the freedom to make what you wish of the assignment. You could take an historical viewpoint, a personal viewpoint, or an omniscient (objective) viewpoint.

PREWRITING

One way to begin is to jot down ideas that come into your head as answers to the question. Look at them and see if there is a relationship among all or some of your ideas. Try to find one sentence which will cover or incorporate all of your related ideas. Then organize your ideas into a logical pattern.

DRAFTING

Your composition should have an introductory paragraph in which you introduce your main idea, your thesis (usually that one sentence that covers or incorporates all of your related ideas). The body paragraphs of your composition should explain and/or develop your thesis. Your concluding paragraph should give your final thoughts on the topic and bring your composition to a close.

PROMPT

When you finish the rough draft of your paper, ask a student who sits near you to read it. After reading your rough draft, he/she should tell you what he/she liked best about your work, which parts were difficult to understand, and ways in which your work could be improved. Reread your paper considering your critic's comments and make the corrections you think are necessary.

PROOFREADING

Do a final proofreading of your paper double-checking your grammar, spelling, organization, and the clarity of your ideas.

LESSON TWO

Objectives
1. To assign speaking parts for the oral reading of the play
2. To preview the study questions and vocabulary for Act 1
3. To practice the speaking part assignments

Activity #1
Assign one speaking part to each of the students in your class. On the page following, you will see a chart listing each speaking part for each act of the play. On the right-hand column in the chart, write the name of the student who will be speaking each part. Either give each student a copy of the part assignment page or post a copy of it where students can see it.

Activity #2
Show students how to preview their study questions and how to do the vocabulary worksheet for Act 1. Give students about ten to fifteen minutes to do the worksheet. Discuss the answers.

Activity #3
Give students the remainder of this class time to look at their parts and to practice reading them orally.

LESSON THREE

Objectives
1. To read Act 1
2. To evaluate students' oral reading skills
3. To give students practice reading orally

Activity
Have students read Act 1 of *A Doll's House* orally in class by doing the speaking parts they were assigned. If you have not yet completed an oral reading evaluation for your students this marking period, this would be a good opportunity to do so. A form is included with this unit for your convenience.

NOTE: If you do not complete the oral reading of Act 1 in class, continue it in Lesson Two. There are too many variables (class ability, fire drills, etc!) to determine exactly how long it will take for the oral reading. Whenever you finish the reading of the act, just go on to do the study questions for that act and then preview the next act, read it, etc.

SPEAKING PART ASSIGNMENTS - *A Doll's House*

Section	Part	Read By	Read By
ACT ONE	NARRATOR		
	NORA		
	HELMER		
	MRS LINDE		
	KROGSTAD		
	RANK		
ACT TWO	NARRATOR		
	NORA		
	ANNE-MARIE		
	MRS LINDE		
	HELMER		
	RANK		
	MAID		
	KROGSTAD		
ACT THREE	NARRATOR		
	MRS LINDE		
	KROGSTAD		
	NORA		
	HELMER		
	RANK		

NOTE: There are 20 speaking parts above. If you have more than 20 students, assign two Narrators, Noras, or Helmers to any or all of the acts. There is an extra column for names of students if you have to (or want to) double-up on parts. Consider assigning students who have trouble reading orally the smaller parts so that they get practice reading but don't get terribly frustrated reading a long part.

ORAL READING EVALUATION - *A Doll's House*

Name _____ Class____ Date _____

SKILL	EXCELLENT	GOOD	AVERAGE	FAIR	POOR
Fluency	5	4	3	2	1
Clarity	5	4	3	2	1
Audibility	5	4	3	2	1
Pronunciation	5	4	3	2	1
_____	5	4	3	2	1
_____	5	4	3	2	1

Total _____ Grade _____

Comments:

LESSON FOUR

Objectives
1. To review the main events and ideas from Act 1
2. To preview the study questions for Act 2
3. To familiarize students with the vocabulary in Act 2
4. To practice reading Act 2

Activity #1
Give students a few minutes to formulate answers for the study guide questions for Act 1 and then discuss the answers to the questions in detail. Write the answers on the board or overhead transparency so students can have the correct answers for study purposes. NOTE: It is a good practice in public speaking and leadership skills for individual students to take charge of leading the discussions of the study questions. Perhaps a different student could go to the front of the class and lead the discussion each day that the study questions are discussed during this unit. Of course, the teacher should guide the discussion when appropriate and be sure to fill in any gaps the students leave.

Activity #2
Give students about fifteen minutes to preview the study questions for Act 2 of *A Doll's House* and to do the related vocabulary work.

Activity #3
Give students any remaining class time to practice their speaking parts. Students who have already completed their speaking parts in Act 1 should study vocabulary.

LESSON FIVE

Objectives
1. To read Act 2
2. To evaluate students' oral reading skills
3. To give students practice reading orally

Activity
Have students read Act 2 of *A Doll's House* orally in class by reading the speaking parts they were assigned.

LESSON SIX

Objectives
1. To review the main events and ideas from Act 2
2. To preview the study questions for Act 3
3. To familiarize students with the vocabulary in Act 3
4. To practice reading Act 3

Activity #1
Give students a few minutes to formulate answers for the study guide questions for Act 2 and then discuss the answers to the questions in detail. Write the answers on the board or overhead transparency so students can have the correct answers for study purposes.

Activity #2
Give students about fifteen minutes to preview the study questions for Act 3 of *A Doll's House* and to do the related vocabulary work.

Activity #3
Give students any remaining class time to practice their speaking parts. Students who have already completed their speaking parts in Acts 1 and 2 should study vocabulary.

LESSON SEVEN

Objectives
1. To read Act 3
2. To evaluate students' oral reading skills
3. To give students practice reading orally

Activity
Have students read Act 3 of *A Doll's House* orally in class by reading the speaking parts they were assigned.

LESSONS EIGHT AND NINE

Objectives
1. To review the main ideas and events from Act 3
2. To discuss *A Doll's House* on interpretive and critical levels

Activity #1
Take a few minutes at the beginning of the period to review the study questions for Act 3.

Activity #2
Choose the questions from the Extra Discussion Questions/Writing Assignments which seem most appropriate for your students. A class discussion of these questions is most effective if students have been given the opportunity to formulate answers to the questions prior to the discussion. To this end, you may either have all the students formulate answers to all the questions, divide your class into groups and assign one or more questions to each group, or you could assign one question to each student in your class. The option you choose will make a difference in the amount of class time needed for this activity.

Activity #3
After students have had ample time to formulate answers to the questions, begin your class discussion of the questions and the ideas presented by the questions. Be sure students take notes during the discussion so they have information to study for the unit test. Because there are so many questions, this unit plan allows for two class periods to thoroughly discuss the answers.

EXTRA WRITING ASSIGNMENTS/DISCUSSION QUESTIONS - *A Doll's House*

Interpretation

1. Write a summary of the main events that take place in the play.

2. Is the story of *A Doll's House* believable? Explain why or why not.

3. Where is the climax of the story? Explain your choice.

4. Are the characters in *A Doll's House* stereotypes? If so, explain the usefulness of employing stereotypes in the play. If they are not, explain how they merit individuality.

5. What is the setting of the play? How important is the setting to the author's theme development? Could this story have been set in a different time and place and still have the same effect?

6. What is the "miracle" Nora waited for "in terror and hope"?

7. What is the "greatest miracle," the one thing that would have kept Nora together with Helmer? Is it likely that it would ever happen?

Critical

8. Describe Nora's relationship with Helmer.

9. Are Nora's actions believably motivated? Explain why or why not.

10. Compare and contrast Nora and Mrs. Linde.

11. Compare and contrast Nora and Krogstad.

12. Explain the importance of Dr. Rank in the play. Why was he included, and what does his presence in the play add to the story and theme development?

13. Explain how the title, *A Doll's House*, is appropriate.

14. Discuss the ideas by which Torvald lives his life. Do they have any merit?

15. Explain how Nora's view of herself changes during the course of the play.

A Doll's House Extra Discussion Questions page 2

16. Define "good marriage" as Nora would.

17. What is Anna-Marie's role in the play?

18. Discuss the roles of heredity and family in *A Doll's House*.

19. Discuss the theme of truth versus lying or appearances in the play.

20. How and why does Nora change during the play?

Quotations

21. Laws don't inquire into motives.

22. I don't know much about laws, but I'm sure that somewhere in the books these things are allowed.

23. . . . most everyone who goes bad early in life has a mother who was a chronic liar.

24. His moral failings I could maybe overlook if I had to--(Helmer about Krogstad)

25. And then to suffer this way for somebody else's sins. Is there any justice in that? And in every single family, in some way or another, this inevitable retribution of nature goes on--

26. Yes--you see, there are some people that one loves most and other people that one would almost prefer being with.

27. Does your husband's love for you run so thin?

28. What's become of the little lark?

29. From now on happiness doesn't matter; all that matters is saving the bits and pieces, the appearance --

30. I've been wronged greatly, Torvald--first by Papa and then by you.

31. Abandon your home, your husband, your children! And you're not even thinking what people will say.

32. I have to think over these things myself and try to understand them.

A Doll's House Extra Discussion Questions page 3

<u>Personal Response</u>
33. Did you enjoy reading *A Doll's House*? Why or why not?

34. Who was responsible for Nora's situation?

35. What makes a good marriage?

36. Based on your knowledge of the characters, what do you think would have happened if Krogstad had gone back and intercepted the letter and had not returned the document?

37. What characteristics does a good husband have? What characteristics does a good wife have?
    What characteristics does a good mother have? What characteristics does a good father have?

LESSON TEN

Objective

To review all of the vocabulary work done in this unit

Activity

Choose one (or more) of the vocabulary review activities listed below and spend your class period as directed in the activity. Some of the materials for these review activities are located in the Extra Activities section in this unit.

VOCABULARY REVIEW ACTIVITIES

1. Divide your class into two teams and have an old-fashioned spelling or definition bee.

2. Give each of your students (or students in groups of two, three or four) the *Doll's House* Vocabulary Word Search Puzzle. The person (group) to find all of the vocabulary words in the puzzle first wins.

3. Give students a *Doll's House* Vocabulary Word Search Puzzle without the word list. The person or group to find the most vocabulary words in the puzzle wins.

4. Use a *Doll's House* Vocabulary Crossword Puzzle. Put the puzzle onto a transparency on the overhead projector (so everyone can see it), and do the puzzle together as a class.

5. Give students a *Doll's House* Vocabulary Matching Worksheet to do.

6. Divide your class into two teams. Use the *Doll's House* vocabulary words with their letters jumbled as a word list. Student 1 from Team A faces off against Student 1 from Team B. You write the first jumbled word on the board. The first student (1A or 1B) to unscramble the word wins the chance for his/her team to score points. If 1A wins the jumble, go to student 2A and give him/her a definition. He/she must give you the correct spelling of the vocabulary word which fits that definition. If he/she does, Team A scores a point, and you give student 3A a definition for which you expect a correctly spelled matching vocabulary word. Continue giving Team A definitions until some team member makes an incorrect response. An incorrect response sends the game back to the jumbled-word face off, this time with students 2A and 2B. Instead of repeating giving definitions to the first few students of each team, continue with the student after the one who gave the last incorrect response on the team. For example, if Team B wins the jumbled-word face-off, and student 5B gave the last incorrect answer for Team B, you would start this round of definition questions with student 6B, and so on. The team with the most points wins!

7. Have students write a story in which they correctly use as many vocabulary words as possible. Have students read their compositions orally! Post the most original compositions on your bulletin board.

LESSON ELEVEN

Objectives
1. To give students the opportunity to practice writing to persuade
2. To have students prepare some materials that they will use in Writing Assignment #3
3. To practice analytical skills
4. To give the teacher the opportunity to evaluate students' writing skills

Activity

Distribute Writing Assignment #2. Discuss the directions in detail and give students ample time to complete the assignment.

LESSON TWELVE

Objectives
1. To give students the opportunity to fulfill the nonfiction reading assignment that goes along with this unit
2. To broaden students' general knowledge about a variety of subjects related to the play

Activity

Explain to students that they will be going to the library to get and read nonfiction articles and books. The articles and books must in some way relate to *A Doll's House*.

Some suggested topics are: marriage, the role of women in society, being a working mother, banking, how to get a loan, Italy, careers in law or banking or home businesses, or articles about *A Doll's House*. A biography about the author would be interesting for some students. These are just a few ideas; any appropriate topic related to the play is acceptable.

Tell students that they are to read nonfiction articles or books and then fill out a Nonfiction Assignment Sheet. Distribute them now so each student has one and then take your class to the library/media center.

LESSON THIRTEEN

Objectives
1. To widen the breadth of students' knowledge about the topics discussed or touched upon in *A Doll's House*
2. To check students' nonfiction reading assignments

Activity

Ask each student to give a brief oral report about the nonfiction work he/she read for the nonfiction reading assignment. Your criteria for evaluating this report will vary depending on the level of your students. You may wish for students to give a complete report without using notes of any kind, you may want students to read directly from a written report, or you may want to do something in between these two extremes. Just make students aware of your criteria in ample time for them to prepare their reports.

Start with one student's report. After that, ask if anyone else in the class has read about a topic related to the first student's report. If no one has, choose another student at random. After each report, be sure to ask if anyone has a report related to the one just completed. That will help keep a continuity during the discussion of the reports.

WRITING ASSIGNMENT #2 - *A Doll's House*

PROMPT

When you go to see a play at a theater, you should dress up a bit and remember your very best manners. When the lights dim, that means the play is about to begin. While the play is in progress, remain in your seat and be quiet. Don't talk, eat, pop gum, or make any unnecessary noise. Having members of the audience making noise and walking in the aisles is very distracting to the actors and to the other people in the audience who want to hear the play. Go into the theater, find a seat, and read your playbill while you are waiting for the play to begin.

The playbill is the program for the play. In it you will find all kinds of interesting information about the play, the actors, and the author. Most people who go to see plays have at least some extra money for entertainment and the "extras" that make life more enjoyable, so it's no wonder that there are usually many advertisements in the playbill as well.

Your assignment is to make two advertisements you think you might find in a playbill.

PREWRITING

First, consider your audience. You have a group of people who usually have extra money to spend on luxuries. Many people who regularly attend the theater are in fact rich. One often sees ads for fine jewelry, real estate, and other high-priced items. Make a list of things you think you might find advertised in a playbill.

The advertisements in a playbill have one purpose: to convince the people who see the ads to buy the products or services offered. We have said that the people have some extra money to spend. What are some other characteristics of theater-goers? Are they usually teens who like rock or rap music or are they a more conservative crowd? If you were to look around the room at the audience, what characteristics would you find? Make a list.

Choose two products and, keeping your audience in mind, sketch out some ideas for advertisements for each of the two products you have chosen.

DRAFTING

Look at your sketches and choose the ones you think are best. Make one good advertisement for each of the two products you have chosen.

PROMPT

When you finish the rough drafts of your ads, ask a student who sits near you to look at them. After looking at them, he/she should tell you what he/she liked best about your work, which parts were difficult to understand, and ways in which your work could be improved. Look at your ads again considering your critic's comments and make the corrections you think are necessary.

PROOFREADING

Do a final proofreading of your ads double-checking your grammar, spelling, and the clarity of your ideas.

NONFICTION ASSIGNMENT SHEET
(To be completed after reading the required nonfiction article)

Name _____ Date _____

Title of Nonfiction Read _____

Written By _____ Publication Date _____

I. Factual Summary: Write a short summary of the piece you read.

II. Vocabulary
    1. With which vocabulary words in the piece did you encounter some degree of difficulty?

    2. How did you resolve your lack of understanding with these words?

III. Interpretation: What was the main point the author wanted you to get from reading his work?

IV. Criticism
    1. With which points of the piece did you agree or find easy to accept? Why?

    2. With which points of the piece did you disagree or find difficult to believe? Why?

V. Personal Response: What do you think about this piece? <u>OR</u> How does this piece influence your ideas?

LESSON FOURTEEN

Objectives
1. To explore the idea of marriage in a practical way
2. To give students some sound advice from an expert
3. To give students the opportunity to ask questions of the expert

Activity

Invite a marriage counselor to your class to talk to students about dating and marriage--things that make a successful relationship and things that are pitfalls. Give students time for a question and answer session after your speaker's presentation.

LESSON FIFTEEN

Objectives
1. To give students the opportunity to practice writing to inform
2. To review the play
3. To give the teacher the opportunity to evaluate students' writing skills

Activity

Distribute Writing Assignment #3. Discuss the directions in detail and give students ample time to complete the assignment.

While students are working on the assignment, call individual students to your desk or some other private area to have a writing conference based on the first writing assignment from this unit. An evaluation form is provided to help you structure your conference if you wish to use it.

LESSON SIXTEEN

Objective
To review the main ideas presented in *A Doll's House*

Activity #1

Choose one of the review games/activities included in the packet and spend your class period as outlined there. Some materials for these activities are located in the Extra Activities section of this unit.

Activity #2

Remind students that the Unit Test will be in the next class meeting. Stress the review of the Study Guides and their class notes as a last-minute, brush-up review for homework.

WRITING ASSIGNMENT #3 - *A Doll's House*

PROMPT

A playbill is the program one receives when one attends a play. It is full of information about the play, the characters, the author, and the actors.

ASSIGNMENT

Your assignment is to design a playbill for *A Doll's House*.

Your playbill should include the following:
A cover (front and back)
A table of contents for the playbill
A brief biography of the author
A short summary of the play
A short analysis of each of the main characters
A program of events showing the order of the acts of the play and the intermission, if any
A list of other works by the author
A summary of the main themes of the play
A summary of the message of the play
The two advertisements you created in Writing Assignment #2
Any artwork, graphics, borders, or pictures which would add to the aesthetics of the playbill

A playbill is often the size of an 8 1/2" X 11" sheet of paper folded in half. This is a good size to make yours.

PREWRITING

The easiest way to begin is to take each item on the list above and outline what will be included in each article/item. This way you can get a feeling for how long each article will be. Then take some sheets of notebook paper and fold them in half and put them inside each other to make a little booklet. Sketch your ideas for how your playbill will appear on these pages. Make a little "mock up" or "dummy" or "rough draft" of your playbill.

DRAFTING

Working from your outlines, write out your articles. When that is done, take clear white paper (typing paper or Xerox paper, for example) and create a rough draft of your playbill, writing in the articles.

PROOFREADING

Have another student in your class read over your rough draft and make comments. Then, make a final, good, clean, perfect copy of your playbill to hand in.

WRITING EVALUATION FORM - *A Doll's House*

Name _____ Date _____

      Grade _____

Circle One For Each Item:

Grammar: corrections noted on paper

Spelling: corrections noted on paper

Punctuation: corrections noted on paper

Legibility: excellent   good   fair   poor

Strengths:

Weaknesses:

Comments/Suggestions:

REVIEW GAMES/ACTIVITIES - *A Doll's House*

1. Ask the class to make up a unit test for *A Doll's House*. The test should have 4 sections: matching, true/false, short answer, and essay. Students may use 1/2 period to make the test and then swap papers and use the other 1/2 class period to take a test a classmate has devised (open book). You may want to use the unit test included in this packet or take questions from the students' unit tests to formulate your own test.

2. Take 1/2 period for students to make up true and false questions (including the answers). Collect the papers and divide the class into two teams. Draw a big tic-tac-toe game on the chalk board. Make one team X and one team O. Ask questions to each side, giving each student one turn. If the question is answered correctly, that students' team's letter (X or O) is placed in the box. If the answer is incorrect, no mark is placed in the box. The object is to get three marks in a row like tic-tac-toe. You may want to keep track of the number of games won for each team.

3. Take 1/2 period for students to make up questions (true/false and short answer). Collect the questions. Divide the class into two teams. You'll alternate asking questions to individual members of teams A & B (like in a spelling bee). The question keeps going from A to B until it is correctly answered, then a new question is asked. A correct answer does not allow the team to get another question. Correct answers are +2 points; incorrect answers are -1 point.

4. Have students pair up and quiz each other from their study guides and class notes.

5. Give students a *Doll's House* crossword puzzle to complete.

6. Divide your class into two teams. Use the *Doll's House* crossword words with their letters jumbled as a word list. Student 1 from Team A faces off against Student 1 from Team B. You write the first jumbled word on the board. The first student (1A or 1B) to unscramble the word wins the chance for his/her team to score points. If 1A wins the jumble, go to student 2A and give him/her a clue. He/she must give you the correct word which matches that clue. If he/she does, Team A scores a point, and you give student 3A a clue for which you expect another correct response. Continue giving Team A clues until some team member makes an incorrect response. An incorrect response sends the game back to the jumbled-word face off, this time with students 2A and 2B. Instead of repeating giving clues to the first few students of each team, continue with the student after the one who gave the last incorrect response on the team. For example, if Team B wins the jumbled-word face-off, and student 5B gave the last incorrect answer for Team B, you would start this round of clue questions with student 6B, and so on. The team with the most points wins!

UNIT TESTS

SHORT ANSWER UNIT TEST 1 - *A Doll's House*

I. Multiple Choice/Identify

____ 1. Nora's husband
      A. Krogstad   B. Helmer   C. Rank   D. Ibsen

____ 2. Author of the play
      A. Krogstad   B. Helmer   C. Rank   D. Ibsen

____ 3. Old friend of Nora; hopes to get a job at the bank
      A. Linde   B. Rank   C. Ibsen   D. None of these

____ 4. Nora borrowed money from him
      A. Krogstad   B. Helmer   C. Torvald   D. Rank

____ 5. Central character of the play
      A. Krogstad   B. Helmer   C. Nora   D. Torvald

____ 6. Has a terminal disease; loves Nora
      A. Krogstad   B. Rank   C. Helmer   D. Linde

____ 7. Nora borrowed money to finance a trip to Italy for him
      A. Krogstad   B. Rank   C. Torvald   D. Linde

____ 8. Nora forged his signature
      A. Krogstad   B. Helmer   C. Rank   D. None of these

____ 9. This was most important to Helmer
      A. money   B. family   C. religion   D. appearances

A Doll's House Short Answer Unit Test 1 Page 2

I. Short Answer
1. What was Nora's secret?

2. How did Krogstad persuade Nora to try to influence Helmer on his behalf?

3. Why doesn't Nora want to see her children at the end of Act One?

4. What was in Krogstad's letter to Helmer?

5. Why did Krogstad send the document back to Nora?

6. Why did Mrs. Linde tell Krogstad not to go get the letter back?

7. What was Helmer's reaction to Krogstad's letter?

8. What did Helmer do when he opened the envelope containing the document from Krogstad?

9. Why did Nora leave Helmer?

A Doll's House Short Answer Unit Test 1 Page 3

III. Composition

What is the point of *A Doll's House*? When we read, we usually come away from our reading experience a little richer, having given more thought to a particular aspect of life. What do you think Henrik Ibsen intended us to gain from reading his play?

IV. Vocabulary

Listen to the vocabulary words and write them down. Go back later and fill in the correct definition for each word.

1.

2.

3.

4.

5.

6.

7.

8.

9.

10.

SHORT ANSWER UNIT TEST 2 - *A Doll's House*

1. Multiple Choice/Identify

    ____ 1. Nora's husband
    A. Krogstad   B. Ibsen   C. Rank   D. Helmer

    ____ 2. Author of the play
    A. Ibsen   B. Helmer   C. Rank   D. Krogstad

    ____ 3. Old friend of Nora; hopes to get a job at the bank
    A. Rank   B. Linde   C. Ibsen   D. None of these

    ____ 4. Nora borrowed money from him
    A. Torvald   B. Helmer   C. Krogstad   D. Rank

    ____ 5. Central character of the play
    A. Nora   B. Helmer   C. Krogstad   D. Torvald

    ____ 6. Has a terminal disease; loves Nora
    A. Krogstad   B. Linde   C. Helmer   D. Rank

    ____ 7. Nora borrowed money to finance a trip to Italy for him
    A. Torvald   B. Rank   C. Krogstad   D. Linde

    ____ 8. Nora forged his signature
    A. Helmer   B. Krogstad   C. Rank   D. None of these

    ____ 9. This was most important to Helmer
    A. Money   B. Appearances   C. Religion   D. Family

A Doll's House Short Answer Unit Test 2

II. Short Answer

1. Describe the relationship between Nora and Helmer.

2. What crime had Krogstad committed, and what was Helmer's reaction to it?

3. Nora was going to ask a favor of Dr. Rank, but she changed her mind. What was the favor, and why did she change her mind?

4. Why did Krogstad send the document back to Nora?

5. Why did Nora leave Helmer?

(Quotations - Explain the significance of the following quotations:)

6. His moral failings I could maybe overlook if I had to--

7. What's become of the little lark?

8. From now on happiness doesn't matter; all that matters is saving the bits and pieces, the appearance--

9. I've been wronged greatly, Torvald--first by Papa and then by you.

A Doll's House Short Answer Unit Test 2 Page 3

III. Composition
1. How and why does Nora change throughout the play?

2. Explain the theme of truth versus lying or appearances in the play.

A Doll's House Short Answer Unit Test 2 Page 4

IV. Vocabulary

Listen to the vocabulary words and write them down. Go back later and fill in the correct definition for each word.

1.

2.

3.

4.

5.

6.

7.

8.

9.

10.

KEY: SHORT ANSWER UNIT TESTS - *A Doll's House*

The short answer questions are taken directly from the study guides.
If you need to look up the answers, you will find them in the study guide section.

Answers to the composition questions will vary depending on your
class discussions and the level of your students.

For the vocabulary section of the test, choose ten of the
words from the vocabulary lists to read orally for your students.

The answers to the matching section of the test are below.

Answers to the matching section of the Advanced Short Answer Unit Test
are the same as for Short Answer Unit Test #1.

<u>Test #1</u>
1. B
2. D
3. A
4. A
5. C
6. B
7. C
8. D
9. D

<u>Test #2</u>
1. D
2. A
3. B
4. C
5. A
6. D
7. C
8. D
9. B

ADVANCED SHORT ANSWER UNIT TEST - *A Doll's House*

I. Multiple Choice/Identify

____ 1. Nora's husband
      A. Krogstad   B. Ibsen   C. Rank   D. Helmer

____ 2. Author of the play
      A. Ibsen   B. Helmer   C. Rank   D. Krogstad

____ 3. Old friend of Nora; hopes to get a job at the bank
      A. Rank   B. Linde   C. Ibsen   D. None of these

____ 4. Nora borrowed money from him
      A. Torvald   B. Helmer   C. Krogstad   D. Rank

____ 5. Central character of the play
      A. Nora   B. Helmer   C. Krogstad   D. Torvald

____ 6. Has a terminal disease; loves Nora
      A. Krogstad   B. Linde   C. Helmer   D. Rank

____ 7. Nora borrowed money to finance a trip to Italy for him
      A. Torvald   B. Rank   C. Krogstad   D. Linde

____ 8. Nora forged his signature
      A. Helmer   B. Krogstad   C. Rank   D. None of these

____ 9. This was most important to Helmer
      A. Money   B. Appearances   C. Religion   D. Family

Doll's House Advanced Short Answer Unit Test Page 2

II. Short Answer

1. By what ideas does Torvald live his life? Do they have any merit?

2. Compare and contrast Krogstad and Helmer.

3. How and why does Nora change throughout the play?

4. What is the "greatest miracle," the one thing that would have kept Nora together with Helmer. Is it likely that it would ever happen? Why or why not?

5. Explain the theme of lying versus appearance in the play.

Doll's House Advanced Short Answer Unit Test Page 3

III. Composition

    The back cover of the Signet Classic edition says this about *A Doll's House*: ". . . brilliantly exemplifies [Ibsen's] landmark contributions to the theater: his probing of social problems, realistic dialogue, and depiction of his characters' inner lives as well as their actions. Rich in symbolism . . . deals convincingly and provocatively with the universal human emotions of greed, fear . . . , and confronts the eternal conflict between reality and illusion."

Defend these statements using examples from the text.

Doll's House Advanced Short Answer Unit Test Page 4

IV. Vocabulary

Listen to the vocabulary words. Write them down. Go back later and use all the words in a paragraph. The paragraph must relate to *A Doll's House*.

A Doll's House Short Answer Unit Test 2 Page 3

III. Composition

Henrik Ibsen wrote *A Doll's House* in 1879, and here we are reading it so many years later. Why? What makes this play a "classic"?

IV. Vocabulary

Listen to the vocabulary words and write them down. Go back later and fill in the correct definition for each word.

1.

2.

3.

4.

5.

6.

7.

8.

9.

10.

MULTIPLE CHOICE UNIT TEST 1 - *A Doll's House*

I. Multiple Choice/Identify

____ 1. Nora's husband
    A. Krogstad   B. Helmer   C. Rank   D. Ibsen

____ 2. Author of the play
    A. Krogstad   B. Helmer   C. Rank   D. Ibsen

____ 3. Old friend of Nora; hopes to get a job at the bank
    A. Linde   B. Rank   C. Ibsen   D. None of these

____ 4. Nora borrowed money from him
    A. Krogstad   B. Helmer   C. Torvald   D. Rank

____ 5. Central character of the play
    A. Krogstad   B. Helmer   C. Nora   D. Torvald

____ 6. Has a terminal disease; loves Nora
    A. Krogstad   B. Rank   C. Helmer   D. Linde

____ 7. Nora borrowed money to finance a trip to Italy for him
    A. Krogstad   B. Rank   C. Torvald   D. Linde

____ 8. Nora forged his signature
    A. Krogstad   B. Helmer   C. Rank   D. None of these

____ 9. This was most important to Helmer
    A. Money   B. Family   C. Religion   D. Appearances

A Doll's House Multiple Choice Unit Test 1 Page 2

II. Multiple Choice

1. True or False: Helmer and Nora have an egalitarian relationship. They both take equal responsibility in earning money and running the household.
    a. True
    b. False

2. What was Nora's secret?
    a. She was starting her own business and was slowly becoming successful. She didn't want Helmer to know about it until she had some profit to show him.
    b. She was pregnant again. She was afraid to tell Helmer because he said he already had enough mouths to feed.
    c. She was secretly in love with another man. She vowed never to act on her feelings because she didn't want to disrupt her family.
    d. She had borrowed the money to finance the trip to Italy to save Helmer's life. She has been making payments by skimming from the household money and taking in copy work.

3. How did Krogstad persuade Nora to try to influence Helmer on his behalf?
    a. He offered her money.
    b. He "sweet-talked" her with compliments about her beauty and her influence over her husband.
    c. He begged her, playing on her sympathy because he was a widower trying to raise his children.
    d. He blackmailed her with his knowledge of something she had done several years earlier.

4. Which of the following is not one of the arguments that Helmer makes to Nora as reasons for firing Krogstad?
    a. Krogstad calls Helmer by his first name at the office, thus reminding everyone of their past friendship.
    b. He has already told everyone that Krogstad will be released.
    c. Krogstad has already secured another position, and it would look very bad for Krogstad if he were to back out on that now.
    d. It would make him (Helmer) look bad to change his mind.

A Doll's House Multiple Choice Unit Test 1 Page 3

5. Why did Mrs. Linde tell Krogstad not to get the letter back?
    a. She thought the secret should be let out of the bag; Nora and Helmer needed to deal with this issue.
    b. It was too late at night and very cold and stormy. Now that they were together again, she didn't want to risk losing him by having him fall ill from the weather.
    c. She thought Torvald should know the truth.
    d. She thought it was too late, that Nora had already picked the lock and taken the letter. Going over now to retrieve it would only make matters worse.

6. What was Helmer's reaction to the letter?
    a. He flew into a rage and called Nora a criminal, a hypocrite, and a liar. He said she was not fit to raise their children and that their marriage would be one only of appearances.
    b. He refused to believe that his "Songbird" would do any such thing. He vowed to get even with Krogstad and have him permanently disgraced so that he would have to move far away if he ever wanted to get work again.
    c. He said he would stand up for Nora no matter what and that he would always love her.
    d. He started crying and then had a stroke.

7. What did Helmer do when he opened the envelope containing the document from Krogstad?
    a. He said it didn't make any difference, that Nora was still wrong, and he would not forgive her.
    b. He instantly forgave her and said that everything would be even better than before because of Nora's weaknesses.
    c. He ran from the room.
    d. He slapped Nora.

8. What did Nora do at the end of the play?
    a. She went to bed and slept happily next to her husband.
    b. She left Helmer to go out and be a part of the world.
    c. She committed suicide.
    d. She begged Helmer to keep her and promised to become a better wife.

9. How does Nora change throughout the play?
    a. She becomes more reserved.
    b. She becomes more independent.
    c. She slowly loses her mind and begins to imagine things that just aren't true about her relationship with Helmer.
    d. She has a couple of affairs but realizes that Torvald is her whole life, so she decides to remain faithful to him in the future. She confesses her affairs before Krogstad blackmails her.

A Doll's House Multiple Choice Unit Test 1 Page 4

10. "Most everyone who goes bad early in life has a mother who's _____."
    a. Uncaring
    b. Over protective
    c. A chronic liar
    d. A kleptomaniac

11. "From now on happiness doesn't matter; all that matters is saving the bits and pieces _____."
    a. for the appearance.
    b. of our marriage.
    c. for the sake of the children.
    d. and forgiving each other.

III. Composition

A Doll's House was written in 1879. What ideas in the book make it seem as if it could have been written within the last twenty years? Explain in detail.

A Doll's House Multiple Choice Unit Test 1 Page 5

IV. Vocabulary - Match the correct definitions to the words.

___ 1. Indiscreet   a. Lacking discretion; not judicious; unwise
___ 2. Hypocrite   b. Prorating or spreading the repayment of debt over a period of time
___ 3. Frivolous   c. Extremely noisy and disorderly
___ 4. Excruciating   d. Lacking abilities
___ 5. Incompetent   e. One who says he believes one way but whose actions show he believes the opposite
___ 6. Capricious   f. Hold off; keep away
___ 7. Vehemently   g. Trivial; silly; unimportant
___ 8. Unperturbed   h. Moved clumsily or stupidly into
___ 9. Interfered   i. Impulsive; whimsical; unpredictable
___ 10. Amortization   j. Extremely attractive
___ 11. Incredulously k. Justly deserved punishment
___ 12. Ravishing   l. Having good manners and social graces
___ 13. Evasion   m. Unruffled; not bothered; calmly
___ 14. Refinement   n. Having declined from a former state
___ 15. Tumultuous   o. Briskly; full of self-confidence
___ 16. Stave   p. Forcefully; full of strong emotions
___ 17. Degenerate   q. Agonizing; painful
___ 18. Blundered   r. Got in the way; hindered
___ 19. Retribution   s. With disbelief
___ 20. Jauntily   t. Act of avoiding

MULTIPLE CHOICE UNIT TEST 2 - *A Doll's House*

I. Multiple Choice/Identify

____ 1. Nora's husband
      A. Krogstad   B. Ibsen   C. Rank   D. Helmer

____ 2. Author of the play
      A. Ibsen   B. Helmer   C. Rank   D. Krogstad

____ 3. Old friend of Nora; hopes to get a job at the bank
      A. Rank   B. Linde   C. Ibsen   D. None of these

____ 4. Nora borrowed money from him
      A. Torvald   B. Helmer   C. Krogstad   D. Rank

____ 5. Central character of the play
      A. Nora   B. Helmer   C. Krogstad   D. Torvald

____ 6. Has a terminal disease; loves Nora
      A. Krogstad   B. Linde   C. Helmer   D. Rank

____ 7. Nora borrowed money to finance a trip to Italy for him
      A. Torvald   B. Rank   C. Krogstad   D. Linde

____ 8. Nora forged his signature
      A. Helmer   B. Krogstad   C. Rank   D. None of these

____ 9. This was most important to Helmer
      A. Money   B. Appearances   C. Religion   D. Family

A Doll's House Multiple Choice Unit Test 2 Page 2

II. Multiple Choice

1. True or False: Helmer and Nora have an egalitarian relationship. They both take equal responsibility for earning money and running the household.
    a. False
    b. True

2. What was Nora's secret?
    a. She was starting her own business and was slowly becoming successful. She didn't want Helmer to know about it until she had some profit to show him.
    b. She had borrowed the money to finance the trip to Italy to save Helmer's life. She has been making payments by skimming from the household money and taking in copy work.
    c. She was secretly in love with another man. She vowed never to act on her feelings because she didn't want to disrupt her family.
    d. She was pregnant again. She was afraid to tell Helmer because he said he already had enough mouths to feed.

3. How did Krogstad persuade Nora to try to influence Helmer on his behalf?
    a. He blackmailed her with his knowledge of something she had done several years earlier.
    b. He "sweet-talked" her with compliments about her beauty and her influence over her husband.
    c. He begged her, playing on her sympathy because he was a widower trying to raise his children.
    d. He offered her money.

4. Which of the following is not one of the arguments that Helmer makes to Nora as reasons for firing Krogstad?
    a. Krogstad calls Helmer by his first name at the office, thus reminding everyone of their past friendship.
    b. He has already told everyone that Krogstad will be released.
    c. It would make him (Helmer) look bad to change his mind.
    d. Krogstad has already secured another position and it would look very bad for Krogstad if he were to back out on that now.

A Doll's House Multiple Choice Unit Test 2 Page 3

5. Why did Mrs. Linde tell Krogstad not to get the letter back?
    a. She wanted to keep it as security. That way, she could never be fired from the bank since she would have the letter to use as blackmail.
    b. She thought the secret should be let out of the bag; Nora and Helmer needed to deal with this issue.
    c. It was too late at night and very cold and stormy. Now that they were together again, she didn't want to risk losing him by having him fall ill from exposure to the weather.
    d. She thought it was too late, that Nora had already picked the lock and taken the letter. Going over now to retrieve it would only make matters worse.

6. What was Helmer's reaction to the letter?
    a. He said he would stand up for Nora no matter what and that he would always love her.
    b. He refused to believe that his "Songbird" would do any such thing. He vows to get even with Krogstad and have him permanently disgraced so that he will have to move far away if he ever wants to get work again.
    c. He flew into a rage and called Nora a criminal, a hypocrite, and a liar. He said she was not fit to raise their children and that their marriage would be one only of appearances.
    d. He started crying and then had a stroke.

7. What did Helmer do when he opened the envelope containing the document from Krogstad?
    a. He said it didn't make any difference, that Nora was still wrong, and he would not forgive her.
    b. He slapped Nora.
    c. He ran from the room.
    d. He instantly forgave her and said that everything would be even better than before because of Nora's weaknesses.

8. What did Nora do at the end of the play?
    a. She went to bed and slept happily next to her husband.
    b. She committed suicide.
    c. She left Helmer to go out and be a part of the real world and become a responsible individual.
    d. She begged Helmer to keep her and promised to become a better wife.

A Doll's House Multiple Choice Unit Test 2 Page 4

9. How does Nora change throughout the play?
   a. She becomes more reserved.
   b. She has a couple of affairs but realizes that Torvald is her whole life, so she decides to remain faithful to him in the future. She confesses her affairs before Krogstad blackmails her.
   c. She slowly loses her mind and begins to imagine things that just aren't true about her relationship with Helmer.
   d. She becomes more independent.

10. "Most everyone who goes bad early in life has a mother who's _____."
    a. Uncaring
    b. A chronic liar
    c. Over protective
    d. A kleptomaniac

11. "From now on happiness doesn't matter; all that matters is saving the bits and pieces _____."
    a. for the sake of the children.
    b. of our marriage.
    c. for the appearance.
    d. and forgiving each other.

III. Composition
   You are Nora writing a letter to Mrs. Linde two months after the play's end. What will the letter say? (Write the letter.)

A Doll's House Multiple Choice Unit Test 2 Page 5

IV. Vocabulary - Match the correct definitions to the words.

___ 1. Tarantella   a. Extremely attractive
___ 2. Seizing   b. Trivial; silly; unimportant
___ 3. Hypocrite   c. Lacking respectability; shady
___ 4. Retribution   d. Moved clumsily or stupidly into
___ 5. Intolerable   e. Agonizing; painful
___ 6. Hysterics   f. Illegal goods
___ 7. Excruciating   g. Unbearable
___ 8. Blundered   h. Having declined from a former state
___ 9. Disreputable   i. Forcefully; full of strong emotions
___ 10. Interfered   j. Got in the way; hindered
___ 11. Suppressing   k. Justly deserved punishment
___ 12. Refinement   l. Prorating or spreading the repayment of debt over a period of time
___ 13. Vehemently   m. Lacking discretion; not judicious; unwise
___ 14. Tumultuous   n. Emotional outbursts
___ 15. Indiscreet   o. Lively Italian dance
___ 16. Ravishing   p. Grabbing; taking & holding
___ 17. Amortization   q. One who says he believes one way but whose actions show he believes the opposite
___ 18. Contraband   r. Holding down or holding back
___ 19. Degenerate   s. Extremely noisy and disorderly
___ 20. Frivolous   t. Having good manners and social graces

ANSWER SHEET - *A Doll's House*
Multiple Choice Unit Tests

I. Matching	II. Multiple Choice	IV. Vocabulary
1. ___	1. ___	1. ___
2. ___	2. ___	2. ___
3. ___	3. ___	3. ___
4. ___	4. ___	4. ___
5. ___	5. ___	5. ___
6. ___	6. ___	6. ___
7. ___	7. ___	7. ___
8. ___	8. ___	8. ___
9. ___	9. ___	9. ___
	10. ___	10. ___
	11. ___	11. ___
		12. ___
		13. ___
		14. ___
		15. ___
		16. ___
		17. ___
		18. ___
		19. ___
		20. ___

ANSWER KEY MULTIPLE CHOICE UNIT TESTS – A Doll's House

Answers to Unit Test 1 are in the left column. Answers to Unit Test 2 are in the right column.

I. Matching	II. Multiple Choice	IV. Vocabulary
1. B D	1. B A	1. A O
2. D A	2. D B	2. E P
3. A B	3. D A	3. G Q
4. A C	4. C D	4. Q K
5. C A	5. A B	5. D G
6. B D	6. A C	6. I N
7. C C	7. B D	7. P E
8. D D	8. B C	8. M D
9. D B	9. B D	9. R C
	10. C B	10. B J
	11. D C	11. S R
		12. J T
		13. T I
		14. L S
		15. C M
		16. F A
		17. N L
		18. H F
		19. K H
		20. O B

UNIT RESOURCE MATERIALS

BULLETIN BOARD IDEAS - *A Doll's House*

1. Save one corner of the board for the best of students' *Doll's House* writing assignments.

2. Take one of the word search puzzles from the extra activities section and with a marker copy it over in a large size on the bulletin board. Write the clue words to find to one side. Invite students prior to and after class to find the words and circle them on the bulletin board.

3. Write several of the most significant quotations from the play onto the board on brightly colored paper.

4. Make a bulletin board listing the vocabulary words for this unit. As you complete sections of the play and discuss the vocabulary for each section, write the definitions on the bulletin board. (If your board is one students face frequently, it will help them learn the words.)

5. Make a bulletin board about women's issues, posting appropriate articles and pictures.

6. Do a fun bulletin board using cartoons which depict the life of a wife, mother, grandmother, etc.

7. Post famous quotes--truthful and/or amusing--about women.

8. Post articles or stories about cases in which the "law" is not "just."

9. Make a bulletin board about careers in the banking industry, the justice system, home businesses, and homemaking.

EXTRA ACTIVITIES

One of the difficulties in teaching a play is that all students don't read at the same speed. One student who likes to read may take the play home and finish it in a day or two. Sometimes a few students finish the in-class assignments early. The problem, then, is finding suitable extra activities for students.

The best thing I've found is to keep a little library in the classroom. For this unit on *A Doll's House,* you might check out from the school library other related books and articles about the role(s) of women in society, characteristics of successful relationships and marriages, law versus justice, morality versus legality, careers in any of the occupations mentioned in the book, or borrowing money. Other plays by Ibsen or a biography would also be appropriate.

Other things you may keep on hand are puzzles. We have made some relating directly to *A Doll's House* for you. Feel free to duplicate them.

Some students may like to draw. You might devise a contest or allow some extra-credit grade for students who draw characters or scenes from *A Doll's House.* Note, too, that if the students do not want to keep their drawings you may pick up some extra bulletin board materials this way. If you have a contest and you supply the prize (a CD or something like that perhaps), you could, possibly, make the drawing itself a non-returnable entry fee.

The pages which follow contain games, puzzles and worksheets. The keys, when appropriate, immediately follow the puzzle or worksheet. There are two main groups of activities: one group for the unit; that is, generally relating to the *Doll's House* text, and another group of activities related strictly to the *Doll's House* vocabulary.

Directions for these games, puzzles and worksheets are self-explanatory. The object here is to provide you with extra materials you may use in any way you choose.

MORE ACTIVITIES - *A Doll's House*

1. Have students create a full production of the play and present it to your school.

2. Have students design a bulletin board (ready to be put up; not just sketched) for *A Doll's House*.

3. Have students write a plot summary of the sequel to *A Doll's House*--what happens to Nora after she leaves Helmer?

4. Use any of the topics mentioned earlier for an in-class library as topics for guest speakers or research papers.

5. Instead of having the groups of students just read the play, have each group actually make a full production of the act assigned. Extra students who do not have speaking parts could be assigned to each group to help with scenery and props.

6. Have students write one of the following letters:
    a. The letter that Krogstad sent to Helmer
    b. A suicide note from Nora to Helmer (the letter she may have left for Helmer had she actually decided to commit suicide) in which she explains why she is committing suicide
    c. A letter which would have been appropriate for Krogstad to include with the document he returned to Nora
    d. A letter which would be appropriate for Nora to send to Krogstad after the end of the play
    e. A letter which would have been appropriate for Krogstad to send to the bank president if he had carried out his threat of blackmail

7. Pose several different scenarios to your students--things that usually cause trouble in marriages --and have students role-play through the scenario trying to find a way to work things out.

WORD SEARCH - *A Doll's House*

All words in this list are associated with *A Doll's House*. The words are placed backwards, forward, diagonally, up and down. The included words are listed below the word searches.

```
W D L P M W V M H L C G I Q R K N P H H L Q L M
H R A J D J G R F N A T Y T L F Y E C E Q C V J
Z P L E U H M E R M S R F L A N M C S F P Q N W
A K R O G S T A D E G R O F B L K N A B L O V E
N C S R H A T L D I F D D M O R Y N L S I S H S
S D T C Y P T I Q C C J N A A S E A A T W D X L
M O T H E R C S C A R I N L S C C T O R V A L D
W V W O P N G D R E H E U E K K O M T C S I L F
V T P Y X Y E O M T R C C S M F O P Z E N L F P
L L J Q G D N L H D C N T A S R P W Y D L C J T
E V B C T H E F L Z A R I P P E M Q E I N Z W Y
F Z J J H H K I H R B L C J X D N T V C N Z J B
L W L V H D H J A S H S G Z D B K I N Q P G G S
Q J K K V C X E X Z P B V M K K J M P G Y T K L
C N D S G M P F W M B X M D K M B X X P N P Q V
K C Q X P P P V J H M W C P H R D G N D A L X F
P B Q D A M X X D T P W M Z C R J V Y T L H L M
```

ACT	HELMER	LINDE	RANK
APPEARANCES	HOPE	LOAN	SCENE
BANK	IBSEN	LOVE	STAGE
BLACKMAIL	ITALY	MORAL	SUICIDE
CHILDREN	JUSTICE	MOTHER	THIN
COPYING	KROGSTAD	NORA	TORVALD
DOLL	LARK	PAPA	FORGED
LAWS	PEOPLE	HAPPINESS	LETTER
	PROMOTION		

CROSSWORD - *A Doll's House*

CROSSWORD PUZZLE CLUES - *A Doll's House*

ACROSS

2. Old friend of Nora; hopes to get a job at the bank
6. Nora didn't want to see hers at the end of Act One
9. Rub to polish; also a light tan color
13. They don't inquire into motives
14. His ___ failings I could maybe overlook if I had to
15. Krogstad wrote one to blackmail Helmer into letting him keep his job
16. Quarters, nickels, dimes & pennies
17. Pretended
18. Extra work Nora took on to help pay off the loan
19. Most everyone who goes bad early in life had a ___ who's a chronic liar
22. At the end of Act Two Nora decided to commit it
23. Indefinite article
24. What's become of the little ____?
26. She borrowed money from Krogstad
28. Coordinating conjunction
29. Nora borrowed money to finance a trip to Italy for him
30. Mrs. Linde gave Krogstad ___ for the future
33. And you're not even thinking what ____ will say
36. Place where a play is put on
37. Play division
38. Nora realized Helmer was more concerned with this than with her
39. Joke with; a small child; a baby goat

DOWN

1. Nora's husband
3. Country where Torvald went to recover
4. Take action
5. And then to suffer this way for somebody else's sins. Is there any ___ in that?
7. Author
8. A ____'s House
10. Nora --- her father's signature on the note
11. Krogstad wrote a letter to ---- Helmer
12. Helmer was expecting one at the beginning of the new year
15. Nora got one from Krogstad
20. Rip
21. Doctor who has a terminal disease
22. Act division
25. Lawyer from whom Nora borrowed money
27. Dr. Rank declared his --- for Nora
31. Krogstad was Nora's --- of money; place where something comes from
32. Concur
33. I've been wronged greatly, Torvald--first by ___ and then by you.
34. Tells an untruth
35. Helmer was to join the ___ right after New Years

CROSSWORD ANSWER KEY - *A Doll's House*

MATCHING QUIZ/WORKSHEET 1 - *A Doll's House*

___ 1. JUSTICE   A. Nora --- her father's signature on the note

___ 2. COPYING   B. Krogstad wrote one to blackmail Helmer into letting him keep his job

___ 3. HELMER   C. Dr. Rank declared his ___ for Nora

___ 4. LOVE   D. And then to suffer this way for somebody else's sins. Is there any ___ in that?

___ 5. BLACKMAIL   E. Nora didn't want to see hers at the end of Act One

___ 6. CHILDREN   F. Play division

___ 7. SUICIDE   G. His ___ failings I could maybe overlook if I had to

___ 8. PAPA   H. At the end of Act Two Nora decided to commit it

___ 9. MORAL   I. Helmer was expecting one at the beginning of the new year

___ 10. ACT   J. Old friend of Nora; hopes to get a job at the bank

___ 11. LOAN   K. She borrowed money from Krogstad

___ 12. DOLL   L. A ___'s House

___ 13. LETTER   M. I've been wronged greatly, Torvald--first by ___ and then by you. you.

___ 14. SCENE   N. Helmer was to join the ___ right after New Years

___ 15. LINDE   O. Nora's husband

___ 16. BANK   P. Mrs. Linde gave Krogstad ___ for the future

___ 17. HOPE   Q. Act division

___ 18. FORGED   R. Krogstad wrote a letter to ___ Helmer

___ 19. NORA   S. Nora got one from Krogstad

___ 20. PROMOTION   T. Extra work Nora took on to help pay off the loan

MATCHING QUIZ/WORKSHEET 2 - *A Doll's House*

___ 1. STAGE A. Krogstad wrote one to blackmail Helmer into letting him keep his job

___ 2. PEOPLE B. His ___ failings I could maybe overlook if I had to

___ 3. ITALY C. Play division

___ 4. IBSEN D. Place where a play is put on

___ 5. PAPA E. And then to suffer this way for somebody else's sins. Is there any ___ in that?

___ 6. LINDE F. They don't inquire into motives

___ 7. JUSTICE G. Old friend of Nora; hopes to get a job at the bank

___ 8. HELMER H. Author

___ 9. BANK I. She borrowed money from Krogstad

___ 10. FORGED J. Helmer was to join the ___ right after New Years

___ 11. SCENE K. Act division

___ 12. MORAL L. A ___'s House

___ 13. TORVALD M. And you're not even thinking what ___ will say

___ 14. SUICIDE N. I've been wronged greatly, Torvald--first by ___ and then by you.

___ 15. NORA O. Nora's husband

___ 16. LAWS P. Nora ___ her father's signature on the note

___ 17. DOLL Q. Country where Torvald went to recover

___ 18. LETTER R. Nora borrowed money to finance a trip to Italy for him

___ 19. ACT S. Extra work Nora took on to help pay off the loan

___ 20. COPYING T. At the end of Act Two Nora decided to commit it

KEY: MATCHING QUIZ/WORKSHEETS - *A Doll's House*

Worksheet 1	Worksheet 2
1. D	1. D
2. T	2. M
3. O	3. Q
4. C	4. H
5. R	5. N
6. E	6. G
7. H	7. E
8. M	8. O
9. G	9. J
10. F	10. P
11. S	11. K
12. L	12. B
13. B	13. R
14. Q	14. T
15. J	15. I
16. N	16. F
17. P	17. L
18. A	18. A
19. K	19. C
20. I	20. S

JUGGLE LETTER REVIEW GAME CLUE SHEET - *A Doll's House*

SCRAMBLED	WORD	CLUE
ALSW	LAWS	They don't inquire into motives
DGFROE	FORGED	Nora _____ her father's signature on the note
ITUESJC	JUSTICE	And then to suffer this way for somebody else's sins
PESIPANHS	HAPPINESS	From now _____ doesn't matter; all that matters if...the appearance--
OGYNCPI	COPYING	Extra work Nora took on to help pay off the loan
INTH	THIN	Does your husband's love for you run so _____?
LAMBALIKC	BLACKMAIL	Krogstad wrote a letter to ____ Helmer
OMALR	MORAL	His _____ failings I could maybe overlook if I had to
EVOL	LOVE	Dr. Rank declared his ____ for Nora
IOORTONPM	PROMOTION	Helmer was expecting one at the beginning of the new year
HIDCENLR	CHILDREN	Nora didn't want to see hers at the end of Act One
ICEUDIS	SUICIDE	At the end of Act Two Nora decided to commit it
CARASPEAPNE	APPEARANCES	Nora realized Helmer was more concerned with his ____ than with her
GETSA	STAGE	Place where a play is put on
RTEOHM	MOTHER	Most everyone who goes bad early in life had a _____ who's a chronic liar
NALO	LOAN	Nora got one from Krogstad
SINBE	IBSEN	Author
LLDO	DOLL	A _____'s House
KRAN	RANK	Doctor who has a terminal disease
RAON	NORA	She borrowed money from Krogstad
NSCEE	SCENE	Act division
EPPLEO	PEOPLE	And you're not even thinking what _____ will say
TTLERE	LETTER	Krogstad wrote one to blackmail Helmer into letting him keep his job
RKLA	LARK	What's become of the little _____?
YALTI	ITALY	Country where Torvald went to recover
GICPNOY	COPYING	Extra work Nora took on to help pay off the loan
APAP	PAPA	I've been wronged greatly, Torvald--first by _____ and then by you
ILEND	LINDE	Old friend of Nora; hopes to get a job at the bank

VOCABULARY RESOURCE MATERIALS

VOCABULARY WORD SEARCH - *A Doll's House*

All words in this list are associated with *A Doll's House* with an emphasis on the vocabulary words chosen for study in the text. The words are placed backwards, forward, diagonally, up and down. The included words are listed below.

```
B X D R T Z F P K K P R T R D N H J K L S Z R M
T S G E X N W H G P L G H G E E X C X Z P X D N
P D U R B K E N Z V X X N G H F G R A B G M H S
H Y P O C R I T E E R C S I D N I E D O M I N O
F J D D L Z U H E A A U O E T E V N N V R F D Y
C R H V I O E T V P P C R N E A R D E E R P X X
F M E E R M V I R P M E Y L T B I E P M R X E K
R S S T E S S I R E F O B S T R E C D K E A D R
R Z G N R H C E R R P A C N U A A D U N R N T Q
M F T N I I S I E F T N Y N R O R B R R U L T E
D L J N O S B T R U N L U L I R U A A I C L R C
Y W G U I I N U P E I M Q Z M Q G T N N D X B C
J T S N V I S E T T T J D B V H G P L T D D E D
X F G G T G R A N I R S C V P R B R K U E J E R
S P K Z H S B U V V O B Y N D Q H C L S M L G N
S V L Y I P A W N E R N W H Z Z Q W S M Q U L C
Q S J D H J V Z X L Z K D Z P T V X S Y S H T A
```

BEDRIDDEN	EVASION	INTERFERED	STAVE
BLUNDERED	EXCRUCIATING	JAUNTILY	SUPPRESSING
CAPRICIOUS	FRIVOLOUS	RAVISHING	TARANTELLA
CONTRABAND	HYPOCRITE	REFINEMENT	TUMULTUOUS
DEGENERATE	HYSTERICS	REPROACH	UNPERTURBED
DISREPUTABLE	INCOMPETENT	RETRIBUTION	VEHEMENTLY
DOMINO	INDISCREET	SEIZING	

VOCABULARY CROSSWORD - *A Doll's House*

VOCABULARY CROSSWORD CLUES - *A Doll's House*

ACROSS
6. With disbelief
12. Prorating or spreading the repayment of debt over a period of time
13. Routine; in a ---
14. Neither's partner
15. Place where Torvald works
16. Holds on to; doesn't give it away
17. What an actor does when he leaves the stage
18. Persuade gently but persistently
19. I've been wronged greatly, Torvald--first by ___ and then by you.
20. Play division
22. Prefix meaning 'against'
24. Thus far
25. Does you husband's love for you run so ___?
26. Nora --- her father's signature on the note
28. Costume with a hooded robe
29. Helmer was to join the ___ right after New Years
30. And you're not even thinking what ___ will say
31. Belonging to me
32. A ___'s House
33. Author
36. Opposite of 'on'
39. Wasting money on extravagant purchases
40. A single
41. One who says he believes one way but whose actions show he believes the opposite
42. Extra work Nora took on to help pay off the loan
44. Opposite of 'closes'
45. Unusual
46. Nora borrowed money to finance a trip to Italy for him
47. Old friend of Nora; hopes to get a job at the bank
48. Doctor who has a terminal disease

DOWN
1. Impulsive; whimsical; unpredictable
2. Illegal goods
3. Hold off; keep away
4. Briskly; full of self-confidence
5. Lacking respectability; shady
6. Lacking abilities
7. Extremely attractive
8. Having declined from a former state
9. What's become of the little ___?
10. Unruffled; not bothered; calmly
11. They don't inquire into motives
21. Nora's husband
23. Extremely noisy and disorderly
27. Lacking discretion; not judicious; unwise
34. Act of avoiding
35. Confined to bed due to illness
37. Trivial; silly; unimportant
38. Nora got one from Krogstad
39. Grabbing; taking & holding
41. Mrs. Linde gave Krogstad ___ for the future
43. Country where Torvald went to recover

VOCABULARY CROSSWORD ANSWER KEY - *A Doll's House*

VOCABULARY WORKSHEET 1 - *A Doll's House*

___ 1. VEHEMENTLY   A. Grabbing; taking & holding

___ 2. RETRIBUTION   B. Prorating or spreading the repayment of debt over a period of time

___ 3. TARANTELLA   C. Unbearable

___ 4. SEIZING   D. Forcefully; full of strong emotions

___ 5. REFINEMENT   E. Having good manners and social graces

___ 6. INCOMPETENT   F. Agonizing; painful

___ 7. JAUNTILY   G. Illegal goods

___ 8. CONTRABAND   H. Having declined from a former state

___ 9. EXCRUCIATING   I. Criticism

___ 10. RAVISHING   J. Extremely attractive

___ 11. HYSTERICS   K. One who says he believes one way but whose actions show he believes the opposite

___ 12. INTERFERED   L. Lively Italian dance

___ 13. CAPRICIOUS   M. Impulsive; whimsical; unpredictable

___ 14. HYPOCRITE   N. Lacking abilities

___ 15. INTOLERABLE   O. Hold off; keep away

___ 16. DEGENERATE   P. Justly deserved punishment

___ 17. SUPPRESSING   Q. Got in the way; hindered

___ 18. REPROACH   R. Holding down or holding back

___ 19. STAVE   S. Emotional outbursts

___ 20. AMORTIZATION   T. Briskly; full of self-confidence

VOCABULARY WORKSHEET 2 - *A Doll's House*

___ 1. Having good manners and social graces
      a. Refinement   b. Tumultuous   c. Bedridden   d. Jauntily

___ 2. Criticism
      a. Refinement   b. Blundered   c. Hysterics   d. Reproach

___ 3. Confined to bed due to illness
      a. Tarantella   b. Retribution   c. Incredulously   d. Bedridden

___ 4. Having declined from a former state
      a. Degenerate   b. Reproach   c. Incompetent   d. Seizing

___ 5. Wasting money on extravagant purchases
      a. Squandering   b. Unperturbed   c. Ravishing   d. Intolerable

___ 6. Trivial; silly; unimportant
      a. Intolerable   b. Frivolous   c. capricious   d. Amortization

___ 7. Got in the way; hindered
      a. Ravishing   b. Interfered   c. Retribution   d. Unperturbed

___ 8. Illegal goods
      a. Reproach   b. Vehemently   c. Interfered   d. Contraband

___ 9. Emotional outbursts
      a. Seizing   b. Disreputable   c. Hysterics   d. Reproach

___ 10. Justly deserved punishment
      a. Retribution   b. Reproach   c. Interfered   d. Squandering

___ 11. Lacking abilities
      a. Indiscreet   b. Unperturbed   c. Incompetent   d. Domino

___ 12. One who says he believes one way but whose actions show he believes the opposite
      a. Frivolous   b. Hypocrite   c. Bedridden   d. Evasion

___ 13. Extremely noisy and disorderly
      a. Capricious   b. Evasion   c. Tumultuous   d. Refinement

___ 14. Unruffled; not bothered; calmly
      a. Squandering   b. Degenerate   c. Unperturbed   d. Seizing

___ 15. Extremely attractive
      a. Tarantella   b. Ravishing   c. Refinement   d. Hypocrite

___ 16. Forcefully; full of strong emotions
      a. Seizing   b. Hysterics   c. Evasion   d. Vehemently

___ 17. Moved clumsily or stupidly into
      a. Blundered   b. Domino   c. Bedridden   d. Incompetent

___ 18. Briskly; full of self-confidence
      a. Hysterics   b. Jauntily   c. Vehemently   d. Disreputable

___ 19. Grabbing; taking & holding
      a. Seizing   b. Interfered   c. Jauntily   d. Degenerate

___ 20. Hold off; keep away
      a. Interfered   b. Stave   c. Ravishing   d. Tarantella

KEY: VOCABULARY WORKSHEETS - *A Doll's House*

Worksheet 1	Worksheet 2
1. D	1. A
2. P	2. D
3. L	3. D
4. A	4. A
5. E	5. A
6. N	6. B
7. T	7. B
8. G	8. D
9. F	9. C
10. J	10. A
11. S	11. C
12. Q	12. B
13. M	13. C
14. K	14. C
15. C	15. B
16. H	16. D
17. R	17. A
18. I	18. B
19. O	19. A
20. B	20. B

VOCABULARY JUGGLE LETTER REVIEW GAME CLUES - *A Doll's House*

SCRAMBLED	WORD	CLUE
UISSNGPPRES	SUPPRESSING	Holding down or holding back
LRDBEDNEU	BLUNDERED	Moved clumsily or stupidly into
MEERETNNFI	REFINEMENT	Having good manners and social graces
YOETRHCIP	HYPOCRITE	One who says he believes one way but whose actions show he believes the opposite
ELRLCUD-ISNYUO	INCREDU-LOUSLY	With disbelief
USRACPOIICC	APRICIOUS	Impulsive; whimsical; unpredictable
THCRSIYSE	HYSTERICS	Emotional outbursts
DRNDBIEDE	BEDRIDDEN	Confined to bed due to illness
QAGIUSENNRD	SQUANDERING	Wasting money on extravagant purchases
EDATPILUERBS	DISREPUTABLE	Lacking respectability; shady
SREDCTENII	INDISCREET	Lacking discretion; not judicious; unwise
EEDIENRRFT	INTERFERED	Got in the way; hindered
USLUMTUUTO	TUMULTUOUS	Extremely noisy and disorderly
ANECGTUXRCII	EXCRUCIATING	Agonizing; painful
LIBETOANLER	INTOLERABLE	Unbearable
ZITTNAAIORMO	AMORTIZATION	Prorating or spreading the repayment of debt over a period of time
EMNELHTYEV	VEHEMENTLY	Forcefully; full of strong emotions
IIZSNGE	SEIZING	Grabbing; taking & holding
RUSOOIVLF	FRIVOLOUS	Trivial; silly; unimportant
BTNREPEUDRU	UNPERTURBED	Unruffled; not bothered; calmly
EGTREANDEE	DEGENERATE	Having declined from a former state
TTNUORERIIB	RETRIBUTION	Justly deserved punishment
EATSV	STAVE	Hold off; keep away
NATLETRAAL	TARANTELLA	A lively Italian dance
CTPENTNIMEO	INCOMPETENT	Lacking abilities
TRONABNADC	CONTRABAND	Illegal goods
IVRGISNHA	RAVISHING	Extremely attractive
LYIJANUT	JAUNTILY	Briskly; full of self-confidence
MIONDO	DOMINO	Costume with a hooded robe

www.ingramcontent.com/pod-product-compliance
Lightning Source LLC
Chambersburg PA
CBHW051419070526
44584CB00023B/3495